T0083664

NATURAL CAUSES

What is the knocking?
What is the knocking at the door in the night?
It is somebody who wants to do us harm.

No, no, it is the three strange angels.
Admit them, admit them.

D.H. Lawrence

ACKNOWLEDGMENTS

The author wishes to thank the editors of the following journals in whose pages many of these poems first appeared:

Barn Owl Review: "The Sweater"; *Connotation Press: An Online Artifact*: "A Late Spring" and "Waterrock Knob"; *Copper Nickel*: "When Everyone I Loved Was Still Alive"; *Cornerstone*: "Housefly"; *Many Mountains Moving*: "Katie by the Sea," "Natural Causes," and "The Clearing"; *Margie*: "Anniversary"; *Minnesota Review*: "On Hearing Congress Has Declared October Sudden Cardiac Arrest Awareness Month"; *The Missouri Review*: "The Gulf," "He Asks the New Owner to Look After His Trees," "Kandahar," "The Man with a Bird's Head," "Nietzsche in Love," and "On Suffering"; *River Styx*: "Browsing the Metaphysical E-Bay Listings, I Find Holy Relics for Sale"; *Waccamaw*: "Two Disused Farms in Kempton, Indiana."

"The Clearing" was also the winner of the 2008 *Many Mountains Moving* Poetry Prize and was nominated for a Pushcart Prize. "At Hank's Canteen" and "Housefly" were awarded a 2008 Dorothy Sargent Rosenberg Award. "Finding the Handwriting of a Woman I Loved in a Paperback She Left Behind Years Ago" was awarded a 2009 Dorothy Sargent Rosenberg Award. "When Everyone I Loved Was Still Alive" was an Honorable Mention for the 2010 Dorothy Sargent Rosenberg Awards.

Grateful acknowledgment is made to the following writers and friends who provided invaluable feedback on many of these poems: Sandra Beasley, Mary Biddinger, Don Bogen, Ben Brown, Matt Burriesci, Bill Coyle, Jim Cummins, Danielle Cadena Deulen, John Drury, Brian Heston, Shanley Jacobs, Aubrey Lenehan, Mari L'Esperance, J. Michael Martinez, Semezdin Mehmedinović, Nancy K. Pearson, Steve Scafidi, Collin Smith, Jack Snyder, Gabriel Spera, Kevin Stoy, Chris Tanseer, Christian Teresi, participants of the Heritage Workshop at George Mason University, and the members of the Portland Accord: Jessica Anthony, Ben Chadwick, Paul Rutz, and Max Stinson. A special thanks to J.D. Scrimgeour and Eric Pankey, *i migliori fabbri*, whose thoughtful comments and suggestions continue to overwhelmingly improve my writing.

I also wish to thank Denise Duhamel for choosing my manuscript for the 2011 Autumn House Poetry Prize, and Michael Simms and the staff of Autumn House Press for all of their blood, sweat, and tears. To my parents Mark and Regina Brodeur, I offer hearty thanks, as well as to my sisters Erin Deslauriers and Courtney Brodeur.

Finally, I owe the most to my dear wife Kiley Cogis Brodeur, without whose love and support this book would have never been written.

In memory of
Major David Brodeur (1976-2011)
United States Air Force
Killed in Kabul, Afghanistan

CONTENTS

The Clearing

3   Natural Causes
5   Anniversary
6   The Gulf
8   Finding the Handwriting of a Woman I Loved in a
      Paperback She Left Behind Years Ago
9   At Hank's Canteen
11 On Suffering
12 The Clearing

Nietzsche in Love

17 Nietzsche in Love
19 On Hearing Congress Has Declared October Sudden
      Cardiac Arrest Awareness Month
20 The Sweater
22 The Tenant
24 Housefly
25 Turtles Hatching
26 Browsing the Metaphysical E-Bay Listings, I Find Holy
      Relics for Sale

Human Services

29 After Rukeyser
30 The Longest Conversation I Ever Had with Yoshi
32 An Incident
33 The Boy Without Arms

34   Human Services

38   Results

40   A History of Violence

The Oldest Living Creature in the World

49   The Man with a Bird's Head

50   The Woman Who Lives Alone

52   Katie by the Sea

55   He Asks the New Owner to Look After His Trees

57   Kandahar

59   Two Disused Farms in Kempton, Indiana

62   A Late Spring

The Foreman's Son

67   When Everyone I Loved Was Still Alive

69   Long Distance

71   The Blizzard of '78

72   The Foreman's Son

75   Waterrock Knob

77   The Student

82   The Grandfather of the Groom Steps Away from the Reception and Talks to His Great-Grandson Asleep in a Pack-and-Play

85   Notes and Dedications

86   Autumn House Poetry Series

THE CLEARING

NATURAL CAUSES

My first week on the job at Sunrise Acres
Miss Ahearn waved me into her room
to share a smuggled pint of apricot brandy.
We sipped from Dixie cups while she told stories:
how she'd never married, graduated
Magna Cum Laude from Wellesley
(she even called herself a "Wellesley Girl"),
how her great grandfather quit the farm at fifteen
and sailed from Belfast to escape the Famine.
I poured myself another, then another,
nodding as she spoke, half-listening,
until she leaned in close and whispered,
"How about a kiss?" I laughed
and took another sip. She placed her cup
on the nightstand by her bed: "Just one kiss?"
I pecked her cheek—figured I owed her
something for the booze—a little surprised
at how coarse her skin was there, how
delicate the bones felt underneath.
Reclining against her pillow, she smiled,
opened her eyes, thanked me, and said politely
if that was all I had then I could leave.
I held my breath and pressed my lips to hers.
She squeezed my nape and slipped me the tongue.
I yanked away, wiped my mouth
and thanked her for the drink. She grabbed my wrist
and grinned. "You won't forget me now!"

Five days later, Miss Ahearn was dead.
The nurse on duty said she must've passed
while she watched her evening shows.

On call that night, I visited her room
before her sister came—we'd been instructed
to leave the body for her next-of-kin.
Alone except for the army of stuffed monkeys
she kept close to her always, cloth baboons
and marmosets worn ragged, she slumped
in her La-Z-Boy with the chimpanzee
she called Nixon (the one without a head).
Another orderly had closed her eyes.
Shy at first, I only glanced at her,
stood by her bed a while, as if waiting
for an invitation to sit. I felt embarrassed
to see her so sprawled out, no longer able
to repair herself in her hand-held mirror.
I kneeled beside her then, let myself stare
as I touched her hand, surprised it was still warm.

I didn't last the month at Sunrise Acres,
left after a double and never came back,
not even to collect my final check.
It's always seemed to me a kind of hell:
to be remembered, yes, but only in fragments
a stranger recollects, sparse episodes
that alter and erase until all that's left
are rows of ragged monkeys missing eyes,
her cheeks smeared pink with rouge,
her last two teeth protruding from her mouth
still gaping as it had for her last breaths.

ANNIVERSARY

A man slides his barstool next to mine, spilling his drink.
He starts to describe the first surge of smoke

he saw through his window at the Embassy Suites Hotel.
And when, he says, he realized some of that office junk

was human beings dropping from the sky,
his first thought was not to run, or even to phone

his wife, but the pair of new binoculars he'd packed.
He focused on one woman, watching her stand on a sill.

Holding someone's hand, she waved goodbye
to those in line behind her, kicked off her heels

and just let go into the weather of that day.
In cargo shorts and tank top, gray curls tucked under

a Red Sox cap, the man looks baleful, ashamed, as he bites
a Marlboro he's been fingering. His palm cups the flame.

He speaks softly, as if consoling a child, offering
no answers, thankfully, as he leans in to confess

it wasn't seeing the towers, or even that falling woman,
but the smell that sickened him, stuck in his throat.

I nod my head, not wanting to turn away.
We sit so close to each other our knees touch.

THE GULF

The lab technician yawns into his mask.
It's late. He hasn't eaten since lunch.
Changing gloves, he makes a small incision
into the sternum of carcass twenty-seven,
a sharp-tooth dolphin who surfaced too quickly.
He slips his hands inside and tries to pull
apart her ribcage as gently as he can,
applying an instrument like an inverted
vise grip, peeling back the layers.
From the hard dorsal aorta, the lack of teeth
in one so young, this cow must've been
the matriarch who led the addled herd
too far off course into the vast network
of Key Largo mangrove swamps
where late-night motorboats struck half a dozen.
He tells me this as I sit watching him,
holding my palm over my nose
against the ammonia odor and fish-rot smell
he says will stay with me for a week.
This is the part of any salvage mission
that makes him wish he'd never volunteered,
when they've saved all the animals
they can, and only a few post-docs linger
to prove what everyone already knows.
He says this animal died of the bends
when a Navy sub tested low-frequency sonar
too close to shore, causing eighty dolphins
to beach off the Marathon coast.
He wonders what the magic number is.
If twenty-five or even thirty dolphins
had beached here would my editor have sent me?

I tell him I don't know. He says he's sorry.
And yet it's obvious he loves this work,
the care with which he moves, how comfortably
the scalpel rests between his index finger
and thumb, an extension of his hand,
how delicately, and with such precision,
he liberates (that's his word, "liberate")
each organ from its cavity before
he places it on a tray, taking the swollen
heart into his hand, the cold weight of it
glinting in the glow of his drop lamp
as he holds it closer to the light to show me.
He makes a fist with his free hand. "You see?
No bigger than a healthy human heart."

FINDING THE HANDWRITING OF A WOMAN I LOVED IN A PAPERBACK SHE LEFT BEHIND YEARS AGO

It must've been our last summer together
when we drank beers on the roof of our two-bedroom
and took the first commuter train

to the Greater Boston Family Planning Center.
The green fluorescents made our faces flicker.
Slumped in a chair, she leaned on my chest and said

"I'm going," and fainted, grinding her teeth.
I didn't know what to do so I stroked her shoulder
as a nurse cracked a capsule of smelling salts.

Next day, the forecast called for rain.
We drove north up 1A to Plum Island
and walked the dunes marked *Keep Off Dunes*

to flush out piping plovers from the beach grass
because she said she wanted to see
something endangered before it disappeared.

We stayed on the shore and watched the storm
drag in off the Merrimac, and dropped to the sand
when lightning struck the spit off Little Neck,

clinging to each other as the squall drenched us,
the tide frothing closer up the beach,
the lighthouse staring seaward with its one good eye.

AT HANK'S CANTEEN

When Hank finds "Digging for Jesus" on PBS,
we watch a dozen pilgrims
squeeze into the underground altar
at the Church of the Nativity in Bethlehem.
They kneel to kiss a polished silver star,
the exact spot where they think Christ was born.

"Crazy what some people will believe,"
says the guy at the end of the bar.
Hank stares at the screen.
"Ever hear of psychic surgery?" the guy asks.
"When I was twenty I was diagnosed
with large-cell carcinoma. They gave me a year.

So I flew to Manila and saw one of those faith healers
force his bare hands between a kid's ribs
and take out what looked like a chicken kidney.
He dropped it in a bucket on the floor
and cleaned the kid off to show there was no wound.
I couldn't go through with it myself.

But when I came home and the head thoracic surgeon
at Boston Medical operated on me
he didn't find anything wrong. No one
could explain it. My tumors had disappeared.
It wasn't that they'd gone benign or something—
they just weren't *there* anymore."

"Bullshit," Hank says. The guy laughs, sips his drink.
Above the register, the boar's head gazes at us.
Someone years ago stuck a cigarette

into one of its nostrils. Under the blinking lights
of the Keno machine, Hank
cranks the volume as loud as it goes.

The TV archeologist says there's no way
to know for sure if Jesus was really born there.
He's standing with the pilgrims in a circle
as they hold hands and sing "Amazing Grace,"
belting the words in different languages
so that the melody is all we hear.

ON SUFFERING

On NPR this morning, a Tutsi woman
says she was five months pregnant

when war broke out, explains how the last
soldier to rape her refused her plea

to shoot, didn't want to waste
the bullet, stabbed her abdomen with his bayonet

and sliced her Achilles tendons
so she could only crawl from the baying strays.

This induced labor, which she tried to stop
by squeezing her legs together, then she tried

to hold onto the child in the wet grass.
But the dogs, she says, the dogs ate my baby.

There's only silence now in the studio.
The woman clears her throat, apologizing—

she doesn't remember what happened next.
Except that when the UN soldiers found her

in the fields beyond her village two days later
and she told her story, they accused her

of lying, of exaggerating her pain.
Two men, she says, lifted her into a jeep

and drove her to the clinic, insisting
that kind of suffering did not exist.

THE CLEARING

I'm thinking of Gidge Tomiolo, the Systems Operator
at the Upper Blackstone Treatment Plant
where I worked part-time the summer I turned sixteen

power-washing the tanks and helping technicians
superheat greywater into pellets
we sold to local farmers as fertilizer.

Gidge would pull up to the dock with another pallet
an assembly line of us loaded on flatbeds, our bodies
forming one concordance in the stink.

I guess a part of me must miss that work,
sweating for minimum wage, scraping nightsoil
from under my fingernails, even the afternoon

I got caught in a downpour doing rounds.
That day, I walked out past the basins,
roamed the woods surrounding the property

and trudged up the gully to watch for deer.
That was when I saw them, two nude figures:
a woman and a man in the clearing,

lying together, their skin turning bright pink.
In the haze, the man looked like—no, *was* Gidge
closing his eyes as he fondled the ample flesh

of the woman straddling him: ten years younger
and (do I have to say it?) not his wife.
I ducked behind a trunk, all three of us

so engrossed we didn't notice
the rumbling above us coming closer, the sky darkening
as the first few drops clicked against the leaves.

So when the clouds cracked open, the downpour
shocked me, sent me hauling-ass
through torrents down the hill, and I remembered

the utility shed I could use for shelter,
an old stone shack of granite and cement.
Shivering under the eaves, I watched the couple

stumble from the woods. Still nude, they carried
their clothes and ran straight toward me.
I tried kicking the steel door rusted shut.

Gidge panted and grinned at me, "Nice day for a stroll!"
As he laughed and smacked the woman's ass,
she dropped her clothes on the steps

and wrung out her dripping hair. She looked at me
then looked at Gidge, picked up her things,
and bunched her sopping blouse against her breasts.

We must've stood so close there out of fear.
I know I was scared when a north-west wind
thrashed the trees, the branches

clattering, and Gidge grabbed the woman's arm
and pulled her closer, told her she'd be warmer
between us two. He put his arm around my shoulders

and squeezed us together, winked at me, still
laughing his belly laugh, his erection
undeniable beside my thigh.

As the woman pressed against me in the heat,
I could feel her trembling, smell the musk
of pine needles and strawberry shampoo

rising from her hair, her skin goose-pimpling
as thunder shook the floor and rattled the panes.
All I could think to do was watch the rain.

Surging across the sky, the lightning revealed
backlit heaves of storm, the bigger gusts
peeling leaves, showing no sign of stopping.

Then it was over. The rain slowed to a piddle.
As he struggled into his pants, Gidge made some comment
that sent the woman stomping off into the woods

gathering both breasts in one hand, her clothes in the other.
We walked back to the Plant together, Gidge
and me, exchanged the odd grunt, but nothing more.

What was there to say? We both were cold, both
hoping to slip in through the loading dock
before the foreman started asking questions.

NIETZSCHE IN LOVE

NIETZSCHE IN LOVE

Strange to think of him as the young professor
genuflecting in some Basel salon
to kiss the hand of Mathilde Trampedach

who giggled into her glove,
her dark hair shining under the oil lamps.
Soon after, he wrote to her from his rented flat,

urging her to gather all the strength
that was in her heart so she would not be frightened
by the question he put to her: would she be his wife?

Though no response survives, we know her answer.
Nietzsche never married, fled to Rapallo
where he sequestered himself in a grand gesture,

letting his moustache burgeon from his face
like a rare fungus. Nor can we blame
Mathilde (nor the others who refused him)

for sparing herself a life with this man
who believed his genius was in his nostrils
and called himself the annihilator par excellence.

So why do I blame her? Eleven years his junior,
she might've seen past his pale complexion
to the Friedrich underneath, who once called love

the most unjust condition in the world.
I like imagining that other Nietzsche:
requited, a family man, too tired at night

to invent the *Übermensch* or kill off God.
Think of the never-to-be-born Nietzsche children—
Frieda and Alastair and little Franz—

squealing as he kneels by their beds, his turn
to read from Mother Goose, which puts them to sleep
faster in French than German. He dozes, too.

Later, he dabs spit-up from his sleeve
as he wanders the Marktplatz, humbled, sober.
Perusing the cobbled stalls for some distraction,

he promises himself he'll write tomorrow
if he tastes one cake tonight, eyeing pastries
on the confectioner's cart, prepared to bargain.

ON HEARING CONGRESS HAS DECLARED OCTOBER SUDDEN CARDIAC ARREST AWARENESS MONTH

Stalled on I-94 outside Bismarck,
I laugh at the AM-station news announcement
that thirty-one days have been dedicated
to the total dysfunction of the human heart.
Indian Summer. What better time to praise the mystery
of the Ford Focus's transmission, the wind thrashing
grit in my eyes, piles of bison shit hardening
on the highway, Coke cans lodged in tufts of prairie grasses
(how long they last out here through so much weather).

Season of Hangovers and Infinite Bliss.
When You Die You Stay Dead a Long Time
Awareness Month. Month of Breaking Down
with a Full Tank in East-Fuck North Dakota
where herds of blackbuck browse over the sage
as the sky flashes and dims, flashes
and dims, nimbostratus pulsing in huge
swells overhead, starting to tap on the hood
and make the asphalt hiss, hemorrhaging rain.

THE SWEATER

Dazed from shoveling snow all day,
I stare a long time at my cardigan

the way one gazes at the ocean or TV.
Though I know its tatty wool has no capacity

to feel pain, doesn't the sweater seem
distraught, fraying beside the winter coats, ragged

with a kind of atrophy? Either way,
it comforts me to think of its sleeves filling

with my absence, cooling with the lack
of my heat. How its shape never quite

forgets me, saves in its yoke the slope
of my shoulders, assuming my poor

posture without judgment or irony.
As I take off my jacket, the sweater stirs a little,

making the hangers chime, swaying in place
like an elderly dancer overcome with

Gershwin. I think I'll bury my face in its folds
and twirl with it a while around the room.

Why not? Don't I owe the sweater
for its fidelity, its years of being forced

to keep so close to me? Each season, its buttons
dangle a little looser and its pockets

sag from the weight of my fists.

THE TENANT

Because this is the fifth Allied National
collection notice I've received
for someone named Raul Ortiz Rodriguez,
I tear open the envelope to see
what he owes, and slice my finger,
smudging Raul's name.

What about you, Raul, my
Camerado, where do you call home?
Moved to the city, maybe, for a job
or to be close to your kids, your second wife
remarried, your black Lab
given away? Maybe, like me,

you were once content to study
the plaster cracking around
the sunken ducts, to lounge in your underwear
and watch another stinkbug drop
from the vent, the chinks in its plated back
splitting open into tiny wings.

It's getting late, Raul. Across the darkening
room, the ancient wall-to-wall
carpeting that must've once
smelled like you, contained your stains,
collects its own shadows
below the digital zero that blinks

on my answering machine.
From the Home Builders Association
Annual Support letters, I picture you

in jeans, your hands powdered
with talc, your workboots trailing pebbles
of dried concrete across the rug

as you press the button of your own machine,
listening to the coldness
of the automated female voice
nagging you to set its time and date,
so inviting, so sure of herself
as she announces: *No new messages.*

HOUSEFLY

Though it's caught between the storm window
and screen, I gaze up every few minutes
to check its progress, admiring

its persistence, the urgency and ease
of its clipped flight. At least the fly has the excuse
of mindlessness for living

recklessly, for coupling in a hurry, abandoning
its young in garbage bins. This thought
depresses me, then the thought

that it doesn't depress me enough
depresses me. I can't help watching the fly
preen its wings on the wire-mesh, proboscis

quivering, as it circles the reflection
of my face and rams its tiny head
into the glass. Crawling across

what we can see of the cumulus outside,
it seems to have finally reached the end
of sky, that blue region where

the vastness of the atmosphere
finds a frame. Thinner than India paper,
its wings blur as it rises to the pane.

TURTLES HATCHING

Justin, the nine-year-old who lives in our triple-decker,
asks if I want to see something wicked awesome
and leads me down the path toward Worcester Sand & Gravel.

Standing over the pit, he points at mayflies
swarming the clutch and says we should find some rocks
and smash the hatchlings to save them from the bugs.

Among track loaders and well drills idling,
they seem too close to earth, smudges of clay
suddenly animated, gleaming as they climb the mud incline.

Justin says there's a pile of stones the construction workers left
when they filled the millpond to build the new high school.
I shake my head and make him cross his heart and hope to die.

An excavator dumps rocks into the circuit crusher
and the ground vibrates through my shoes.
The hatchlings' bodies steam. Only a few have cleared

the crest of the nest, toppling down, scaling the steep
ditch walls, each thorny carapace teeming over
the other, their claws the size and shape of caraway seeds.

Grappling for a purchase in the sand, they scrabble
their separate paths out of the pit, their faces
blunt and striving, stippled with grit.

BROWSING THE METAPHYSICAL E-BAY
LISTINGS, I FIND HOLY RELICS FOR SALE

A college friend who'd saved ten years
of his toenail clippings in a mayonnaise jar
calls tonight to tell me his wife

gave him an ultimatum: *the jar or me.*
He says he thinks the counseling is working.
The second honeymoon to Puerto Vallarta.

Best, he says, to stick it out for the baby,
and I get a hollow, kicked-in-the-stomach feeling.
It's okay, he says, we Catholics believe

everything broken will be made whole again
in heaven. I laugh. He laughs louder.
I joke about how Saint Philomena's teeth

are going now for thirteen-hundred each,
asking him if he knew that when Philomena's grave
was found nine centuries after she died

the blood inside an urn set by her tomb
was still moist. Here's what I know, he says:
There are no words between two people

that won't be misconstrued, corrupted, lost.
Some nights, he says, he lifts the covers,
slides in beside her, and feels her belly

rise and fall. Sometimes she squirms
against the coldness of his fingers.
Sometimes, still asleep, she touches back.

HUMAN SERVICES

AFTER RUKEYSER

"I lived in the first century of world wars."

I lived in the second century of world wars.
I woke each day and dry-swallowed my pills
for hypertension and high cholesterol
and turned on my devices asleep on the desk
to check the nighttime progress of the wars.
It was like peering underneath a bandage
at a wound that would not heal. I waited
for myocardial dysfunction or septic shock
to put an end to them. But the wars
only changed names, addresses, currencies.
I thought about the periods between wars
when munitions are stockpiled in storehouses
and the civilian population can forget.
Then an unmanned drone missed its target
and blew up another crowded marketplace
and I braced myself to feel the repercussions
and felt no repercussions. I took issue
with the Democratic Party's war-time positions
and voted Republican then I took issue
with the Republicans and voted Democrat.
I tied a yellow ribbon to a poplar tree.
I drove the long way home and sat in traffic
in front of Sunrise Assisted Living
and gazed into a window facing the street
at a figure in a cotton gown and thought:
Human beings live too long today.
I lived in the second century of these wars.

THE LONGEST CONVERSATION
I EVER HAD WITH YOSHI

Leaning against the fence between our yards,
he asks if I've ever heard of Olkiluoto,
an uninhabited island in the Baltic

where the Finnish government stores copper canisters
of nuclear waste. He says they don't know how long
the canisters will stay radioactive,

if a million years is optimistic or not,
but the good news is most scientists agree
civilization will end before we find out.

I haven't heard. He asks me what's the single
greatest achievement of Western Culture, what could outlast
Mount Rushmore, the Parthenon?

Shakespeare? I say, Dante Alighieri?
He laughs and shakes his head. Nuclear waste.
Imagine, he says, some future nonhuman race

excavating that site in search of clues
of who we were, digging up those tunnels
and prying open the canisters we couldn't label

dangerous in a way they'd understand.
Years later, they'll climb into the light
with artifacts, and wonder why they're dying

by the hundreds, then the thousands.
Snipping his shears, Yoshi spits on the grass
and walks the gravel path to his nasturtiums.

I stay a while longer by the fence, watching him
spray aphids from the shield-shaped leaves, the gray
fangs of his beard widening as he smiles.

AN INCIDENT

I wanted to call the cops and just keep walking
but my wife protested, so I knelt beside the man
sprawled on the sidewalk, and cupped his neck in my palms,
and lowered his head from where he must've fallen
against a planter, and laid him flat on his back.

It was late. The streetlamps gleamed on the damp road.
He looked up at me and tried to speak,
his mouth sealed on one side, his eyes alive
with fear as he grunted and spat on himself and me.
"Should we be moving him?" my wife asked.

I glared at her, "Don't you have your phone?"
and she dialed, not knowing how to answer the dispatcher's
What happened? How old? Any medications?
His feet were wrapped in Safeway bags
and he wore a winter coat, though it was June.

I slid a hand under his head to cushion him
from the pavement, and held my other hand
over his face, keeping the rain out of his eyes.
Glancing down 17th every few seconds, I thought:
I've never touched a black man's hair before.

The EMTs pulled up, lifted him onto a gurney,
and clattered him into the back. They didn't thank us.
The engine idled, filling the air with exhaust.
When they drove off without a siren,
I wiped my hands on my jeans.

THE BOY WITHOUT ARMS

From the Metro station, he steps into the sun,
his sleeves cut off, his hands dangling

directly from his shoulders, stiff, unfinished.
His hair is parted, clean. His pristine sneakers

are double-knotted, his shirt tucked into his jeans.
Who helped him dress this morning?

He turns around and looks into the crowd.
I see her now, she's there, the caregiver, a woman

following behind him to help him feed his change
into the SmarTrip card machine for bus fare—

his mother by the same soft slope of the nose, the same
spattering of freckles on her cheeks, the thoughtful

distance she keeps between them, giving him
room, but watching him and watching the others

pass him on the curbside as he stoops
to press the crosswalk button with his chin.

HUMAN SERVICES

1.

The night Collin borrowed the group-home van
to pick me up from T. F. Green, he brought
Cindy along for the ride—I didn't know why.

Cindy would get this galvanized look in her eyes
and just start smacking staff, slapping whoever
tried to keep her from hurting herself or others.

We could only restrain her, stay out of her way.
Collin, the night manager, had a system.
Whenever Cindy started whaling on us,

he'd stand behind her and grab her left arm
with his right, her right arm with his left,
so she made a crosswise X, hugging herself,

and he'd hold her tight like that until she settled
and we could pump her full of Klonopin.
The slightest nudge could set her off again.

At T. F. Green, I found them at baggage claim
by the baby grand the airport paid musicians
to play on busy travel days. Behind them,

a piano tuner was tweaking the strings,
making high-pitched upward-climbing notes
that must've addled Cindy. Near the escalators,

she made her mean face and refused to move.
So Collin fished around in his coat pocket.
"Cindy," he said, "Look, Cindy, want this penny?"

and he flashed a coin in front of Cindy's face.
"Come on," Collin said, backing away,
and Cindy followed us out the door.

   2.

Sometimes we got lucky—sometimes not.
One Paddy's Day, her mother called to tell me
she couldn't make the drive from Leominster.

I was alone on duty, trying to finish cooking
a corned-beef dinner and get them all in bed.
Cindy wouldn't come out of her room.

When everyone was bathed and fed and sleeping,
I opened Cindy's door. She stood there naked,
grinning like she'd been bad, the blazing floor lamps

showing her ribs protruding, her C-section scar.
I asked if she was ready for her shower
and led her by the wrist into the bathroom.

As I turned the water on, she stepped into the tub.
"Too cold," she said, so I flipped the nozzle up.
"Too hot! Too hot!" I told her it was fine.

She shook her head and wouldn't clean herself.
I rubbed soap on the facecloth and scrubbed her neck.
She grinned and held herself with both hands

then stepped out of the stream, squatted,
pissed on her hand and smacked it in my face.
"Fuck you!" I screamed and threw the soap at her

as she laughed—I couldn't believe it—she laughed at me.
"Know what's funny?" I said, "Your own mother
abandoned you here because she never loved you.

No one ever loved you and no one will
because you're crazy and ugly and disgusting
and you're going to die here miserable and alone."

3.
I only crossed the line one other time.
I'd spent the night again in Whitinsville
and drove to work to start my day shift early.

Unlocking the basement door to relieve Collin,
I noticed the staff daybed was still made,
and thought maybe he'd crashed on the couch.

Climbing the carpeted stairs to the second floor,
I heard a woman grunting down the hall.
"Cindy?" I said, "are you okay in there?"

and pushed open the door. Her room was dark.
From the sunlight seeping in between the blinds,
I could see two figures. "Get out!" Collin said.

In a white t-shirt and socks and nothing else
he stood with his back to me, his bare ass showing.
"Sorry," I said, and ran back down the stairs.

When Collin showed himself, I was washing dishes.
"Listen," he said, "I don't know how it happened" . . .
"Just leave," I said, and gazed into the sink.

He swung open the front door. "Don't worry," he said,
"she's on the pill." I could see his bald spot gleaming
as he turned to go then turned around again.

"You know," he said, "you may not appreciate it.
But this is going to help her in the end."
He grabbed his bag and clicked the front door shut.

RESULTS

Mounted on the exam-room wall, a TV flashes
CNN footage of baby Jessica,
the eighteen-month-old in Midland Texas
who fell into a well over twenty years ago.
Now, at twenty-five, married, the mother of a son,
she's just inherited a million-dollar trust fund.
Doctor Salbert breezes into the room
and spreads my labs out on his lap to show me

it's benign. I don't know what to say.
I sit there grinning as he pats my knee.
"Relax," he says, "My job is to *prevent* disease
not to treat you when you're lying on your deathbed."
He points at the TV. "It's like Jessica—
If her parents would've kept the back door shut
she never would've found that open well."
He plugs his stethoscope into his ears.

The TV shows Jessica strapped to a stretcher,
her face blank with an animal exhaustion
as she rises out of the shaft at the end of a guy wire
into a flickering world of camera crews.
Gliding past hardhats, her skin smudged with mud,
she doesn't look human at all, but like some hybrid
scientists had lowered to let us know
if hell was safe for human exploration.

Salbert rises to scrub his hands, spattering foam.
Through missing slats in the blinds, I can see
bare branches trembling against the glass,
birds jostling for the last berries

as Salbert scribbles on his pad, his mouth
gaping in concentration, his chipped tooth showing.
"See you in eight weeks," he says, "okay?"
I keep nodding after he turns away.

A HISTORY OF VIOLENCE

1.
I'd never seen her so fired-up before.
Staggering to the couch, my mother-in-law

wedged herself between us and said it was time
we knew the truth about Amy's estranged father,

and told us about the night he came home late
and she confronted him about his drinking.

She said he'd lost his license the week before
and had to walk the two miles home from Leverett,

taking the short-cut trails around Pine Hill,
so when he opened the door his clothes were soaked.

Charlotte was precise with her description
of where she said he could stick his apologies,

how sick she was of him, how physically ill
she became when he touched her, when he spoke.

2.
Our first few years together before Amy
we were happy. We watched TV in bed

sprawled head-to-foot and tickled each other's feet
to see who could go longer without flinching.

We both agreed we never wanted kids.
But around year three I felt a change inside me.

When I started buying children's clothes at Penney's
and hiding them in bags under the stairs

he found them and asked me whose they were.
I told him they were mine—ours—for the baby.

What baby? he said. He slammed the door.
I didn't see him for three days after that.

3.

She said she was holding Amy—a baby then—
when she started shoving him with her free arm,

following him into the den, calling him worthless.
He hadn't touched her since Amy was born.

So he took her by surprise when he shoved her back,
and she hit her head on the mantelpiece.

She came after him then with a fire poker
and jabbed at him. Again, he pushed her,

hurling her back this time across the room
against the fire-guard and into the fire.

Charlotte said she could smell her hair burning
as she leapt out of the embers, still holding Amy,

who wouldn't stop crying.
Her husband cried, too, apologizing,

and later claimed she must've tripped over
the toys she'd left on the floor.

4.

It wasn't his violence I hated most
but the words he spoke after to console me

the honey baby please he thought would help.
Or the way he looked at me with his half-smile

saying I didn't know how much he loved me
and that he'd never raise his hand again.

The first few times my mother took me in
and told me I could always come home

but she changed her mind when she married Steve.
Steve said I must've done something wrong

to make him hit me with a closed fist
and my mother started to agree

saying I needed to practice temperance
and shut my mouth when he came home like that.

5.

How many people disappear each year?
Even today, in the backwoods of this country,

how many sites exist where a woman
could bury the body of her husband?

I'm thinking of the woods behind Charlotte's house
that buffer the Quabbin from Route 202.

When I first moved to Barre, I didn't know
four towns had been flooded to make the reservoir,

that the Swift River had been impounded
and buried the cellar holes of demolished houses.

From Charlotte's woods, you can still walk down
dirt roads that lead straight into the water.

One August, when it hadn't rained in weeks,
I thought I saw a church spire poking through

the surface of the Quabbin, an old cast-iron
crucifix protruding, rusted, bent.

6.
The year Amy was born our marriage turned.
Garbage dirty laundry pots and pans.

He started spending more time in Leverett.
I had my daughter. Why shouldn't he be happy too?

One night while he was out I found his keys
in the jeans pocket he wore the day before

and I didn't bother to unlock the deadbolt.
He pounded at the door slurring his words

and didn't look at me when I let him in.
I remember thinking he wasn't drunk enough

to start a fight but he pushed me to the floor
and kicked me in the stomach and fell on me

and spread my legs out under him and tore
my underwear and told me I liked it rough

and I screamed for him to get the fuck off me
and he laughed and told me to hold still.

7.

When she saw him bleeding on the bedroom floor,
she was shocked at how much blood

spilled out of his body, his human body,
how small he looked curled up against the wall

as he whimpered, twitched, and went unconscious.
She said you can still see the spot on the hardwood

where he stained the grain. But, once, when she wasn't there,
I flipped back the rug and couldn't find it.

I'm not saying Charlotte killed her husband,
but I don't know if I believed her when

she said he slept it off on the bedroom floor
and left early the next day and never came back.

   8.
I don't know why he did but he got off me
and stood above me and said he was sorry

in that condescending tone and left the room.
He was taking off his pants in the bedroom

when I flipped the light and kicked his bad knee
and he fell on his ass saying what the fuck

and I started laughing at him as he tried to stand.
I turned away and grabbed a snowglobe

off the bedside table and broke it across his head
and threw my lamp at him and a framed picture

and a coffee mug and told him to eat shit
and he collapsed with glass shards in his hair.

   9.
When I asked Amy if she believed her mother,
she said she did—what else could she believe?

But I'm not sure myself what really happened.
Once, walking the woods behind Charlotte's house,

I found a rhododendron in a clearing
where pines had matted the sod with coppery needles

that choked the light so nothing else could grow.
Rain had dissolved the snow and the new buds

hesitated, blooms splitting the branches
and turning pink, but only barely pink.

Scanning the muddy ground for anything green,
I felt my feet sinking into the needles

as I stood beside the bush. It looked planted.
Who'd plant a rhododendron in the woods?

Lifting in the wind, the leaves revealed
their undersides. I touched the cold branches

and I wasn't sure if the bush had given up
or if it simply waited to be coaxed.

THE OLDEST LIVING
CREATURE IN THE WORLD

THE MAN WITH A BIRD'S HEAD

He's the only human likeness at Lascaux,
a bird-man stick-figure lying prostrate
on the cavern wall, dead or playing dead,

beside a crouching bison and a spear.
Our guide, Marcel, tells the tour in English
the artists saw each figure in the rock

before they painted them, each stag and stallion
suggested in formations already there,
and simply traced the outlines with a horsehair brush.

"Not art for art's sake," Marcel muses,
"they painted what they loved to hunt,"
which explains the bear and oxen, aurochs, goats.

But the man? Huddling up to see
the squiggle curving upward from his waist
like an erection, we point and kick

each other's heels, asking questions
we know we'll never have the answers to.
The floor sweats, smutted with a dank musk.

Half-blind under track lights, we squint
at cracks in the calcite, whispering.
Our voices echo louder than we mean.

THE WOMAN WHO LIVES ALONE

for Anne Mulinax Jones

He plants the raccoon traps where she tells him to,
drops the gauge-wire cages by her nibbled
cabbages, and trails through the mulch
the meatball bait they made out of peanut butter
and cat food, climbing her sunroom stairs
to see if they can catch them pilfering.

Inside, he finds the bathroom, locks the door
and washes his hands with the bottled cleanser
she asked him to use so he wouldn't ruin
the sea-shell soaps she bought at Yesterday's Rose.
He glances above the mirror at snapshots
of her modeling days, dusty black-and-whites

of a woman smiling in a two-piece bathing suit.
She's waving to the camera. She must be twenty.
Tendrils of damp hair stick to her shoulders,
her lips full and painted, the creamy flesh
of what he can see of her breasts gleaming with wet.
She calls for him. He says he'll be right there.

Filling his glass with white-zin from a box,
she urges him to stay as she squeezes the spout
with her arthritic fingers, two copper rings
covering her thumbs, one twisted pinky
cocked at the knuckle to forty-five degrees.
Would he care for another plate of casserole?

Her garden buzzes now with insect noises,
cicadas hissing, crickets in the hostas.
When he tells her he has to go, she shushes him—

she rolls her eyes and actually says "shush,"
asking what she's supposed to do without him
if the raccoons come tonight, if she catches one?

They sit back in their chairs, listening
for the high-pitched cries or the rattling of cages,
as the sun sinks behind the tulip poplars
bordering the wetlands to the west,
making them look like shadows of themselves,
black figures swaying in the darkening room.

KATIE BY THE SEA

Her half-brother speaks.

1.

On her beach towel, two tie-dyed dolphins breach.
I tell her about the real dolphins I saw
on a deep-sea fishing trip with Dad last year.

I got one once, I say, a female rough-tooth,
to eat straight from my hand. Its body glowed.
Its grainy tongue looked bigger than a cow's.

She laughs. I like her laugh. Last night, we watched
two male dolphins on the Nature Channel
keep a female hostage, take turns with her

so no others could have her—she wanted others.
Each time she tried to escape, thrashing
free, they'd butt their bottle-noses into her.

Katie didn't like to see her hurt. I told her violence
is a part of nature. She laughed. I like her laugh.

2.

Dad doesn't think I know how it happened,
but I have ears. He says Katie's mother's
piece-of-shit boyfriend found her

hanging from an orange extension cord
tied to the basement rafters, took what cash
she kept around the house, panicked, and called Dad.

Dad says she still looked pretty dangling there,
dressed in a tank top and cotton panties,
thick strands of black hair sticking to her face.

At first, Dad wanted nothing to do with Katie.
"I'm sorry," he'd say, "but that girl's mother
was a piece of shit. Her kid can't be much better."

But when she acted out at supper, he never hit her.
He must've gotten used to her, I guess.

3.
One summer, he paid for her gymnastics.
He'd smoke and watch her practice in his workroom.
Rewinding her cassettes, he'd make her dance

faster and faster, yanking on her ankles
when she tried to do the splits on the concrete floor,
holding her down until she got it right.

She showed me once where Dad hid his rubbers.
We blew them up like balloons, two at a time,
sending them sputtering out his bedroom window.

At first she didn't want to run away.
She'd get confused. I'd tell her she was too big
to climb in bed with me, that it wasn't right.

She'd laugh at me and say, "This is *our* bed,"
and she'd end up sleeping with me anyways.

4.

In the surf tonight, she finds a dried stingray.
"It's funny how they drown in air," she says,
"how death makes them not scary anymore."

"Turn your head one way," I say to her,
"and you can hear the sea, turn the other way
and the wind keeps imitating the sound of the sea."

She turns, she listens, but all she says she hears
is the sound of my voice echoing in her ears.
The tide's gone oily now in the drowning sun.

It surges up the shore and bubbles back,
spewing froth all over our sandy feet.
She sits between my knees. Her hair, tied back,

whips my face, thick as a barber's brush.
I squeeze her hand and feel her squeezing back.

HE ASKS THE NEW OWNER
TO LOOK AFTER HIS TREES

I mean that stand of pitch pines off the garden.
They were planted in the nineteenth century.
Sometimes I'd imagine myself caretaker
of pines in the White Mountains of California,
those ancient great-basin bristlecones.

Ever seen what four thousand years looks like?
My wife Jenna and I drove west one spring
to hike Inyo, and saw Methuselah,
the oldest living creature in the world.
We couldn't look at it for very long.

Gnarled and knotted in the stony ground,
it only resembled a living thing.
When illness forced Jenna into bed,
she looked unreal, as if an artist
who'd never known her had carved her out of wood.

Do you have a wife? I didn't think so.
The week I buried Jenna at Saint Brigid's,
I gave her clothes away to Salvation Army.
What they wouldn't accept I brought out back
and doused with kerosene in an oil drum.

I thought of taking pity on my trees
and burning them to their roots, digging up what's left
and burning that too, burying the ashes.
I couldn't bring myself to do it, though.
Pitted in the drifts, they were glazed with glass.

Their needles ticked and shivered in the cold.
I stayed so long I couldn't feel my feet.
You'd think I was tapped. I even talked to them.
I pressed my face into their fragrant branches
until my beard was sticky with pitch.

KANDAHAR

I drove to Jacksonville to see my son
before he deployed with Echo Company.
He stood on the hotel bed with his boots on

and shouted, "This is my rifle, this is my gun,"
and laughed as we cracked our cans together.
Seeing his grown-up body hard from Basic,

I was proud—I'd never served myself.
But later that night, his hands shook so bad,
he could hardly deal for a game of Spit.

I told him everything would be alright.
What else could I say? His eyes were wild,
his scalp all sandpaper without his curls.

At home, I keep a framed picture of him
on my desk in his old room, an office now.
Leaning against a Jersey barrier,

he smiles with his helmet on, his face peeling,
his teeth stained yellow from the cigarettes.
Because he took the photograph himself,

the shot's crooked, his long forearm extending
out of view. Behind him, razor wire
scraping the sky, planes floating in the blue.

Last time I heard from him he said he was calling
from Kandahar. But where is Kandahar?
I tried looking it up on the computer.

All I found were facts, history.
Soon after the DOD knocked on my door,
I woke one night and roamed the empty house

and found myself downstairs in his old room,
flipping the light to make sure he was there.
Seeing his bed replaced by cardboard boxes,

I panicked for a second, then I remembered.
At my desk, I looked hard at his picture
for something new, some small detail I missed.

TWO DISUSED FARMS
IN KEMPTON, INDIANA

1.

I remember the story my mother-in-law told me
about the farm adjacent to her own.
A granary and house in disrepair, a polebarn

crumbling, reduced to a woodrot heap
built too close to what became Route 28.
From Bonnie's front porch, you can still see

the sunken roof decaying, the rafters now
exposed, stubble fields surrounding lopsided stables
punctuating the space between horizons.

A woman lived there alone on twenty acres.
She had a son, I think, but something happened.
Cancer or a wreck—I don't remember.

Once, close to the time when the woman died,
Bonnie, who was paid to clean her house,
lugged over her bucket of supplies, pushed open

the door, and watched the woman fall
out of her chair and kneel at Bonnie's feet,
asking her if she was the angel of death.

Next morning, Bonnie woke to the sound of singing.
Following the voice into the fields,
she found a set of footprints in the snow

and saw the woman muttering by the woodshed,
her eyes closed, hair tangled in rosethorns,
lying in her nightgown on the ice.

Unable to move when Bonnie tried to lift her,
the woman spat in Bonnie's face, still singing
what sounded like a garbled version of

"He's Got the Whole World in His Hands."
Bonnie waited with her until the ambulance
drove up the berm to carry her away.

2.
That was almost thirty years ago.
Bonnie's own farm now is in disrepair.
When Grace and I drive up to spend the night,

we find her gazing out the picture window,
pointing at some recent aspect of decay.
The increased angle of the tower silo

shedding its planks and boards along the field,
rust crusting the dome, the staves splitting,
the ruined tractor she stacks with potted plants

and paints green every Spring to hide its age.
Since Bonnie bought a gun, a twenty-two
she keeps in the nightstand by her bed, loaded,

we've started stopping over twice a week,
saying we'd been to Tipton for the day
at Wal-Mart or United Methodist.

Chain-smoking her Montclair 100's,
she says she has an angel watching over
and slaps her black lab's belly with a hairbrush.

Her angel, Bob, the dog, is deaf and blind.
Hearing a noise one night, Bonnie cocked her pistol
and stumbled over him, discharged a slug

into the player piano, destroying the action.
Next morning, when she didn't answer her phone,
I drove up to check on her. I knocked and knocked.

Because she'd nailed a quilt above the door
against the drafts, I had to tear it down,
scattering drywall on the floor where I found her.

As I helped her up, she told me not to fuss,
she preferred the rug some nights for her slipped disk,
and licked her fingers to fix her sticky hair.

A LATE SPRING

From my porch chair, I watch house finches
squabble at the feeder for the last
kernels of thistle seed, warring cheerfully
for the topmost perch, little flecks
of rust flaking from their play.

Or is it serious? Since Saturday,
the finches have devoured thirteen pounds
of sunflower. Now they're demanding more.
So I pour my own concoction into the tube,
which they seem to enjoy: peanuts and Fruity Pebbles.

I imagine them incredulous at first, their bills
inquiring over the crushed-up grains
before they dig in, learning to love the strange bounty
like the growing Beijing middle class
who've cultivated a taste for Pizza Hut.

Once, I tried a handful of raw millet
and spat it back in the sack, too bitter for me.
I wanted to taste the staple of this species
who escaped from New York cages in the 1930s.
I think of them invading Mastic Beach,

breeding poolside, harrying the rich
who cursed them as they poisoned heated bird baths
and hired men to hose shit off their roadsters.
Which is one explanation for why the finches flee
from the slightest movement, refusing my palm.

They don't trust me. Who could blame them?
But they need my charity in this bare season
before the flowers fill the air with seed,
and so they accept without question
whatever crumb I toss them, tearing

apart the crust of a stale bran muffin we share.
Flittering on the eaves, the finches agree
(their fleet song says as much—*agree agree*), one call
chasing another, all appetite,
as they pipe above me, twittering, nearly free.

THE FOREMAN'S SON

WHEN EVERYONE I LOVED
WAS STILL ALIVE

Playing foot-soldier by the run-off brook,
I tore branches from pines, my "dynamite"
I chucked into the shallows and watched explode,

and found the carcass of a Canada goose
decaying in the weeds where one branch landed.
I kneeled and poked at the goose with my stick

until I was convinced it wouldn't move.
Feathers tattered, neck kinked back, its ribs
were exposed, clean as piano keys.

I wedged both hands beneath it, pressed its body
to my chest, and draped its bloated neck
over my shoulder so it wouldn't dangle,

and carried it up the gully through the woods.
At my back door, I called for my mother
and asked as she approached if she could fix it.

She screamed, smacking the goose out of my arms,
stripped me naked and drew a scalding bath
to scrub the goose-rot from my hands and face,

scolding me for mucking around with dead things.
After scooping the goose off the patio floor
with two dustpans she wielded in either fist,

she shoveled a hole behind the rusty swings
and let me say a prayer as we buried it.
Two days later, I took my father's spade

and dug up the goose, shocked to see its body
flat and black, its wings and waddled feet
a mass of feathers I couldn't get untangled,

and brought it back inside to show my mother
who spanked me, told me I knew better,
and pitched it in the trash, a brick on the lid.

Why couldn't I leave the goose carcass in peace,
let it rest there on its bed of sunken cattails
where it chose to lie, if the goose could choose,

lured, I guess, by the sound of water,
its wings folded neatly at its sides,
its head bowed to the stream as if to drink?

LONG DISTANCE

I have to talk to you about your mother.
The other night she got a little crazy
and drove home from O'Malley's on her own
and when the garage-door opener wouldn't work
she decided to take a nap in the driver's seat.

I was playing cards at the VFW.
Around midnight, I got a call from the people
we sold the old house to, telling me
your mother was in their drive, intoxicated.
She'd driven to the wrong house.

"Gina, Gina," I said, "get up, they're going
to call the cops." She was so out of it.
Twice we had to pull over on 290.
She opened the door and leaned outside
and would've taken a header on the asphalt

if I hadn't grabbed her by the belt.
Bright and early, she was up with coffee,
waiting for me to drive her to Shrewsbury
to pick up her car. I sat her down at the table
for a little talk. Well, I talked, she listened.

*

Don't people ever just talk to each other?
I'll tell you what my father never told me.
Your life isn't your own. You close your eyes
and wake up forty, married, unemployed.
Or maybe you're employed—that's even worse.

You feel divorced from life, estranged, a stranger.
You grab the wheel and downshift into neutral
and watch the windshield blur, the streetlights streak.
If you're lucky, you have a sense of your destination.
But when you arrive it's never how you pictured.

The boutique hotel room has filthy carpet
and the toilet won't stop flushing. You lift the lid.
What do you know about indoor plumbing?
You peer into the water and touch the valves.
Go on. Jiggle it. See if it stops.

THE BLIZZARD OF '78

I was 3 months pregnant. I barely made it home from work,
and couldn't shovel. 3 teenage boys
took 2 days to dig me out so I could pack
a bag and my cats and walk to my parents' house
about 1½ miles away. Dad was stuck on a major highway

in R.I. He had to walk 10 miles to get to shelter.
On the way, he and others were knocking on car windows
to get people out so they wouldn't freeze to death.
Him and about 200 others stayed in a local church.
The Red Cross gave them bologna for a week.

I finally heard from Dad about 3 days after the storm.
Grandpa drove me down to go get him.
He was in the same clothing for a week. I was working
for the state then. I licensed day care facilities.
The state closed all offices for the entire week.

There were no cars except for emergency vehicles
and snowmobiles allowed on the streets.
It was great to be walking around Main Street
and the people out were all so friendly and helpful.
I felt like we moved back in time. 6 months later

you were born. The Blizzard is so vivid it seems like it was
last year. Now you're almost 30 and I'm 60!
You're always asking about what happened then so here it is.
You'll probably change everything like you always do.
But I hope you don't. Remember. Tell the truth.

THE FOREMAN'S SON

Weekdays without a sitter, dad put us to work
banging nails into junk sheetrock

or fetching a Phillips or a ball-peen hammer
from the toolbox he kept tied to the flatbed.

That morning, my sister stayed in the truck.
I remember Dad standing on plywood slats

and arguing with the guy delivering siding
when my sister kicked the stick shift into neutral

and the truck went rolling backwards down the hill
and bucked up the curb onto the sidewalk

and hit the framed house across Wadsworth.
The pickup stopped against a finished wall.

One of the crew, a painter, reached her first.
He opened the door and lifted her from the cab

as Dad and I booked across the lot
and he tore my sister from the man's arms.

Holding her, Dad felt for broken bones,
found none, and shook her hard, asking her

what was she thinking, she could've been *hurt*.
My sister hung limp in his arms, not even crying.

Dad looked at the painter, another Guatemalan
he called "Mexican" who wore baggy jeans

and a backwards baseball cap under his hardhat.
His thin mustache looked like a caterpillar.

"Don't you *ever* touch my daughter," dad spit.
The painter wiped his face. "Es'cuse me, sir?"

"You heard me." "Nothing, I did nothing, sir."
Dad set my sister on the seeded lawn.

"You fuck," he said, shoving the painter,
who stumbled toward the new foundation next door.

Dad shoved him again, sending him staggering
backwards through the caution tape, which snapped

as the man lost his balance, fell six or seven feet,
and landed with a thud on the muddy ground.

Dad gasped—I don't think he'd seen the hole—
holding out both hands toward the painter

as if warming them against an open flame.
I remember thinking the man was dead,

that my father had *killed* someone, and I was scared
when the man in the foundation opened his eyes

and propped himself on one elbow, resurrected.
"Get up," my father said, "get off my lot

or I'll call the cops. Hear me? *La policía?*"
The painter stood and slapped dirt from his jeans.

Across the street, the crew smoked, watching us.
Dad kicked an empty joint-compound bucket.

Sitting my sister on his lap, he said he loved her.
The sore under his eye where a yellowjacket

had stung him when he'd tried to spray its hive
had opened again. I leaned against his shoulder.

My bare arm touched the thick hair of his forearm.
"You're fine," he said. "It's okay, you can cry."

WATERROCK KNOB

In the lot outside the Sylva Waffle House,
they talk about their options for the day,

deciding on a drive up the Blue Ridge Parkway.
Their rented Saturn putters as they climb

from four to seven thousand feet. They gape
at stone outcrops and ledges of sheer

granite disappearing into the mist.
Across the valley, fog swallows the peaks.

He slows to twenty-five and tries to follow
the solid yellow line along the asphalt.

"Where are we going?" she asks, "are you okay?"
He sees a sign for Waterrock Knob Trail

and parks beside a two-tone Ford Bronco
with Tennessee plates, the hood caked with rust.

From the gravel lot, he can barely read
Waterrock Knob Summit: 0.9 Miles,

the sign spattered with moon-mushrooms of lichen.
Loping up the trail, he passes her, stepping

over stones, spillage from the crumbling
ridge-spine. And this becomes their pattern:

He cuts in front and rounds a bend of wind-
dwarfed pines, stops to wait for her,

and lets her pass, then overtakes her again,
never allowing her to catch her breath.

Snowflakes sting their faces on the slope.
"Don't go so fast," she says, "I don't feel well."

"We're almost there," he says. She clutches her stomach.
"I really have to go. I'm serious."

"Go where?" he says, realizing what she means.
She walks behind a boulder off the trail.

"Keep watch," she shouts, "just make sure no one comes."
He wipes the condensation from his glasses.

Upwind from where she'd slipped into the thicket,
he sniffs the foul odor of something human

and looks both ways along the path. Nothing.
He searches for her figure in the mist,

but the cliffs, the trees, even his feet have vanished.
He thinks of the Bronco in the parking lot.

How long had it been parked there?
Behind him, a crackling of branches.

He shivers in his coat. "You almost done?"
The world around him has no form, no color.

Holding out both arms in front of him,
he edges through the fog, calling her name.

THE STUDENT

1.
I met her at the library where she worked.
Wide at the neck, her blouse exposed one shoulder

so that when she turned to pull my book
from the Hold shelf, I could see

the prolific freckles on her back,
a pentacle tattoo at the nape of her neck

where a man with a goat's head mounted a woman
whose limbs were knotted like the limbs of trees.

I made sure I was last to leave that evening.
When she locked up, I asked to bum a Parliament

and we talked a while beside the bus shelter.
I came back every night for the next two weeks,

chatting with her at the Circulation Desk.
Then, one night, as we stood on the library steps,

she said she thought she'd missed the 12:15
and asked if I would mind walking her home.

Cutting down Ocean Ave, we shared a flask.
I tasted cherry lip-gloss on the spout

as the hulls of deck boats on the cove knocked
like elevator doors against the docks.

2.

Five flights up, her apartment stank of sage.
Her lampshades, draped with fake-silk kerchiefs,

made her teeth glow green as she smiled at me
and scooted closer on the folded futon.

She asked if I believed in the Triple Goddess.
"The Gods are real," she said. "They're not people

like you and me, they're instruments of power."
As she reached over my legs to open a drawer,

I felt her heavy breasts brushing my thigh.
It took me a moment to see she was holding

a knife the size of an envelope opener,
a dagger double-edged and carved with glyphs.

"Don't be afraid," she said, "it's not for cutting."
"What's it for?" I said. She grinned, "I'll show you."

3.

Next morning, I woke alone on her floor.
The sun through the blinds threw slatted bars of light

across the hardwood covered with cat hair.
I gathered my clothes and made my way back home

to my sublet behind the double smokestacks
of Pacific Gas & Electric's coal-burning plant.

In the shower, my neck stung under the spray.
The water at my feet was tinged with pink.

I remembered the dull blade on my skin,
the feel of cold metal across my back,

her knees pressing down against my wrists
as she sat on me, not letting me turn over.

The whole week after, I kept finding marks
scabbed on my back and shoulders, tiny nicks

I'd glance in the bathroom mirror when I shaved.
They seemed to reveal themselves only

gradually, darkening before they crusted over,
itching as they healed. Then they were gone.

   4.
Soon after I spent the night at her apartment,
I took the commuter train back home to Worcester.

As usual, I found Dad in the kitchen,
the box fan blasting as he smoked his menthols,

his oxygen tank on wheels next to his chair.
I asked if he still had my boy-scout knife.

He said he must've pitched it with the clothes
my mother left when she moved in with Gene.

I spent the day down cellar searching boxes.
Dad kept shouting down the stairs for me.

After an hour or so, he finally joined me.
I'd taken off my t-shirt against the heat.

"What's that?" he said, pointing at my scabs.
"What's what?" I said. He stood there, smiling.

    5.
That was the last time we spoke to each other.
After calling for three days with no response,

my brother Terry drove to Grafton Street
and found him slumped on the toilet,

a bowl of seedless grapes spilled on the floor.
At the funeral, I was furious at Dad

for letting himself die the way he did.
Sweating in the pews, I clenched my teeth.

After the service, we headed to Dad's house.
Standing in the room Dad never used,

I watched our relatives scarf chicken salad.
I wanted to yell at my brother to shut up

and stop telling his friends how Dad had died.
"Grapes?" they'd say, choking back a laugh.

My brother would shrug, "All old people think
they're constipated, even if they go once a day."

6.

I saw the woman once more after that.
Taking the long way home one night, I climbed

the stairs of the library. She wasn't there.
So I staggered down Derby Street and stood outside

her building on the sidewalk, watching her windows.
She'd left the blinds open and I could see

her figure kind of drift from room to room.
Pausing at one window, she gazed out

or gazed at her reflection—I couldn't tell.
I groped forward and stumbled over a planter

and reached for a chip of cobble at my feet
and threw it, striking the bricks under her sill.

She stepped away. In the dark, I gathered
rocks, but every one I tossed missed the glass.

I wanted her to see me so I moved closer,
walking into the road under the streetlamp

to chuck them harder and with more conviction,
pitching them upward, aiming for the light.

THE GRANDFATHER OF THE GROOM
STEPS AWAY FROM THE RECEPTION
AND TALKS TO HIS GREAT-GRANDSON
ASLEEP IN A PACK-AND-PLAY

I've always preferred funerals to weddings.
The food tastes better and everyone tells
fond stories about the one in the box

no matter what they thought of him in life.
I never knew my second cousin Ding
earned a Purple Heart in the Pacific.

Ding, who made himself a paraplegic
driving home one night from Finder's Pub
and killed a teenage girl in a station wagon

and would've gone away a long time
if his father hadn't been a Town Selectman.
Even in that chair, Ding had a nasty streak.

We all saw how he treated his wife Pammy.
Put her in Saint Vincent's more than once.
She'd say something Ding didn't like

and he'd haul off and belt her where she stood,
whacking her in front of the family
or in line at Walgreens—he couldn't care less.

The man had no control. But that afternoon,
I watched Pam and the kids weep by his coffin,
nodding when the priest called him a hero.

It's different when the one who dies is young.
I'm thinking of your cousin Sarah Anne,
Mag and Teddy's girl. She had the sugar.

At age thirteen, she fell into a coma
and never woke up again. Teddy and Mag
would stay with her in twenty-hour shifts.

Mag had already lost her job at Zayres
and Teddy had to take a second mortgage.
That was one funeral I wish I'd missed.

My father-in-law, Red, is another story.
Playing eight-ball at Stoney's once, Red called
two Army Privates on leave "baby killers."

He couldn't have been a day under seventy.
They would've killed him if I hadn't intervened.
I cracked a pool cue across one guy's face

as Red sat smiling. I felt awful, but Red was family.
Last time I set foot in the old man's house
my son Mark, a toddler, was throwing his food.

I gave him a smack, my son, a tap on the hand.
Red screamed at me, "If you touch my grandson again
I'll kill you." I grabbed Red by the collar

and slammed him up against the Frigidaire,
his feet dangling as I lifted him higher,
his glasses clattering to the hardwood floor.

When he died, I nearly crapped myself laughing.
Still, at dinner, after we buried him, I cried.
I couldn't help myself. I lied and said

how much he'd meant to me, a second father.
Stone-cold sober, I had to leave the room.
I don't know why I put on such a show.

I guess it comes from growing old yourself
and watching too many of your friends go.
Then, one morning, you hop out of the shower,

wipe steam from the mirror, and realize
you've outlived your own father by thirty years.
Thirty years. He wouldn't recognize me.

My face scrunched like newspaper in a fire.
Everything *like* and nothing as it was.
You'll see. You'll live forever just like me.

NOTES AND DEDICATIONS

The book's epigraph comes from "Song of a Man Who Has Come Through," *The Complete Poems of D. H. Lawrence* (Heinemann, 1964).

"Natural Causes" is in memory of Lillian Reynolds (1916–2007).

"Nietzsche in Love" owes much to Rüdiger Safranski's *Nietzsche: A Philosophical Biography* (Norton, 2002), translated by Shelley Frisch.

"After Rukeyser" is written after "Poem," which appears in *The Collected Poems of Muriel Rukeyser* (University of Pittsburgh Press, 2005).

"Kandahar" is for Matthew and Kevin Stoy.

"Two Disused Farms in Kempton, Indiana" is for Bonnie Wolfe and Lynn Cogis.

"Long Distance" is for Mark Brodeur, with apologies.

"The Blizzard of '78" is for Regina Brodeur.

"The Grandfather of the Groom Steps Away from the Reception and Talks to His Great-Grandson Asleep in a Pack-and-Play" is for Matt Burriesci, who is responsible for the first line.

THE AUTUMN HOUSE POETRY SERIES

Michael Simms, General Editor

OneOnOne / Jack Myers
Snow White Horses / Ed Ochester
The Leaving / Sue Ellen Thompson
Dirt / Jo McDougall
Fire in the Orchard / Gary Margolis
Just Once, New and Previous Poems / Samuel Hazo
The White Calf Kicks / Deborah Slicer • 2003, selected by
  Naomi Shihab Nye
The Divine Salt / Peter Blair
The Dark Takes Aim / Julie Suk
Satisfied with Havoc / Jo McDougall
Half Lives / Richard Jackson
Not God After All / Gerald Stern
Dear Good Naked Morning / Ruth L. Schwartz • 2004, selected by
  Alicia Ostriker
A Flight to Elsewhere / Samuel Hazo
Collected Poems / Patricia Dobler
The Autumn House Anthology of Contemporary American Poetry
  / Sue Ellen Thompson, ed.
Déjà Vu Diner / Leonard Gontarek
lucky wreck / Ada Limón • 2005, selected by Jean Valentine
The Golden Hour / Sue Ellen Thompson
Woman in the Painting / Andrea Hollander Budy
Joyful Noise: An Anthology of American Spiritual Poetry
  / Robert Strong, ed.
No Sweeter Fat / Nancy Pagh • 2006, selected by Tim Seibles
Unreconstructed: Poems Selected and New / Ed Ochester
Rabbis of the Air / Philip Terman
The River Is Rising / Patricia Jabbeh Wesley
Let It Be a Dark Roux / Sheryl St. Germain
Dixmont / Rick Campbell
The Dark Opens / Miriam Levine • 2007, selected by Mark Doty
The Song of the Horse / Samuel Hazo

My Life as a Doll / Elizabeth Kirschner
She Heads into the Wilderness / Anne Marie Macari
*When She Named Fire: An Anthology of Contemporary Poetry by
American Women* / Andrea Hollander Budy, ed.
67 Mogul Miniatures / Raza Ali Hasan
House Where a Woman / Lori Wilson
A Theory of Everything / Mary Crockett Hill • 2008, selected by
Naomi Shihab Nye
What the Heart Can Bear / Robert Gibb
The Working Poet: 75 Writing Exercises and a Poetry Anthology
/ Scott Minar, ed.
Blood Honey / Chana Bloch
The White Museum / George Bilgere
The Gift That Arrives Broken / Jacqueline Berger • 2009, selected by
Alicia Ostriker
Farang / Peter Blair
The Ghetto Exorcist / James Tyner*
Where the Road Turns / Patricia Jabbeh Wesley
Shake It and It Snows / Gailmarie Pahmeier*
Crossing Laurel Run / Maxwell King*
Coda / Marilyn Donnelly
Shelter / Gigi Marks*
The Autumn House Anthology of Contemporary American Poetry
2nd edition / Michael Simms, ed.
To Make It Right / Corrinne Clegg Hales • 2010, selected by
Claudia Emerson
The Torah Garden / Philip Terman
Lie Down With Me / Julie Suk
The Beds / Martha Rhodes
The Water Books / Judith Vollmer
Sheet Music / Robert Gibb
Natural Causes / Brian Brodeur • 2011, selected by Denise Duhamel

• Winner of the annual Autumn House Poetry Prize
* *Coal Hill Review* Chapbook Series

DESIGN AND PRODUCTION

Cover and text design by Kathy Boykowycz
Cover painting: "Belief in the Afterlife" by Bo Bartlett

Text set in Minion, designed in 1990 by Robert Slimbach
Titles set in Skia, designed by Matthew Carter

Printed by McNaughton and Gunn on Glatfelter Natural, an FSC
certified paper.